DREAM-DROPS & DOODLES ON OKRA

An Immersive Poetry Collection for Big Kids

Bea Ngozi Udeh

Published by Big White Shed, Nottingham, England 2019
ISBN 9781916403536
Copyright © Bea Ngozi Udeh

Printed and bound by Booksfactory EU

Cover design Bea Ngozi Udeh
Illustrations by Amanda Williams

A CIP catalogue of this book is available from the British Library

A note or two on this creative collection of words - poetic, prose and mumblings from my head.This collection is about relationships and kids; of kid's relationships with big people and big people engaging with life. This collection is about self-care and their care-raising awareness for what you ignore to acknowledge.

Sometimes we forget to engage with a moment when we are in it, or to reflect on that moment that caused us to well up with a feeling of discomfort or luxurious joy. I have been very lucky to land some of these poems in different spaces and places as readings or as performance poetry. I experience the impact of them on you in those moments and way after. We, the big people, forget the impact that we have on kids in the spaces that we occupy or force them to occupy. Some of us are lucky to be big kids and to play. I thank the universe that I learn from my kids everyday in a way that makes me know myself better.

So, I am trying to ensure that everything in this collection of work can be discussed, taken apart or enjoyed for the page and spoken and shared in kitchens, living rooms, classrooms, unusual habitats and staged settings.

I am using the language of parents and carers who live in me, dine with me and of the kids who have trodden on my head, as well as the inner child who beckons me to share these narratives from inside my head. My collaboration with Creative Artist, Amanda Williams, has provided some cool spaces for you to read, reflect, doodle and write. I am in awe of writer, theatre director and performance artist, Kat Francois' work ethic and her honesty when she agreed to edit this collection. Some of this might seem really simple and some of it may even be quite clever, but I want for you, the reader, the big kid to read, drop dreams, doodle and enjoy.

Contents

Daughter

A response to the Highlife song Sweet Mother
by Prince Nico Mbarga and Rocafil Jazz.

In memory of our girls in Chibok

I am the eldest daughter
of the eldest daughter
of the eldest daughter.
Of a village in Eastern-Nigeria. From Eastern Igboland

I have given birth to many children who fill my hair
with the beautiful orangeness of the dust
and the greys of multiple miscarriages.

I can account for each follicle on my scalp
for the thick skin that passes sweat
as I think of how I laboured
suffered so that I hoped you would not suffer.
But I miss you
and I will rip two hundred and thirty four follicles from my scalp
each day until you return to us.

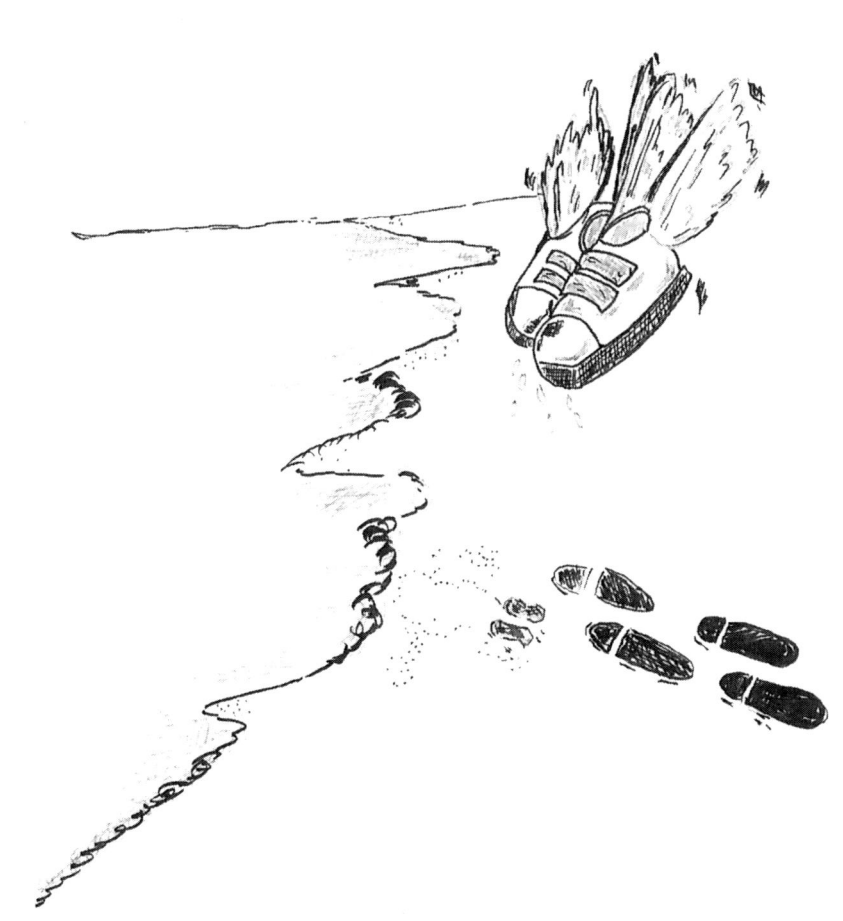

Beach Boy

in memory of Alan Kurdi

Scroll up.

Pink high-heeled shoes.

Smiley. Pout at digital camera.

Instant graphics of dimples

embedded in thigh blubber

leaning forward for England

arse way behind in Nigeria

scrolling endearments like a pet lover.

Scroll up. Pause.

But loving

is a laptop dropped on its side

the motherboard waiting to be wiped

of pixelated memories

too old for makeup. Nevertheless

experienced at cropping

her top into a Marvel game avatar.

Scroll up.

She-Hulk.

Red,

wrestles with Ferrari Theft Auto

strong enough to transport your sins

to a God who carries dead children

like toys and tosses them onto

a Top 10 Turkish beach

abandoned.

Yet everybody longs to hold him in their cold embrace.

Pause.

And I wish that I owned a toy like that

when I was younger.

Dressed simply in t-shirt rouge

a pale Syrian rag doll with dark hair

navy Velcroed shorts

and limp arms outstretched.

Scroll up. Zoom in.

And those shoes.

Ready.

Sturdy

Back to school black

I've bought similar on Ebay

I've shared my rejects on Freecycle

and I want to breathe life into you.

Pause.

Want to

Scroll.

Want to

Stop.

Want to

force your spirit into one of those boxes

that hold reasons to be cheerful grids

ticked to make my discomfort

at ogling at your prone being

a thing to stand up for

a gift toy to die for

I ignore the 'Like' button

and scroll on.

warrior women

Warrior Women

We are women warriors

Arriving in Derby by boat upon the shores of Alvaston with honour
in our chests

Rattlesnakes tremble alerting a choir of Billies and Chavs, tempers
steaming, worries breathing.

Releasing petals of strength as rare as the chocolate cosmo, we

Instantly quell their regrets.

Our stories are shared over fired-meat seasoned with chilli-sauce
and flat bread pizzas

Right-left-right is the rhythm of our songs as we work magic into souls.

Spears aloft, we warrior women shine hope into the sockets of bats.

Concrete

I was first moved by poetry

When the hearts of my twin first borns

Shuddered to stillness in my hands

After sucking in their last breaths

I was nearly moved by poetry

When my Uncle wrote me a love poem

Begging my forgiveness

For the misappropriation of my youth

I was nearly moved away from poetry

When they stuffed mics down my oesophagus

Disrupting my passion to air my voice.

So, I turned off the radio to broadcast my own affirmations

I am always moved by poetry

When my youngest child

Says I love you

For holding his jabbed hand during brain investigations

I seek truth and justice in poetry

Reconnecting lost rhythms with rainbows, yet,

Avoiding sharing the Talk with my African British sons

As they transition into tomorrow's gentlemen.

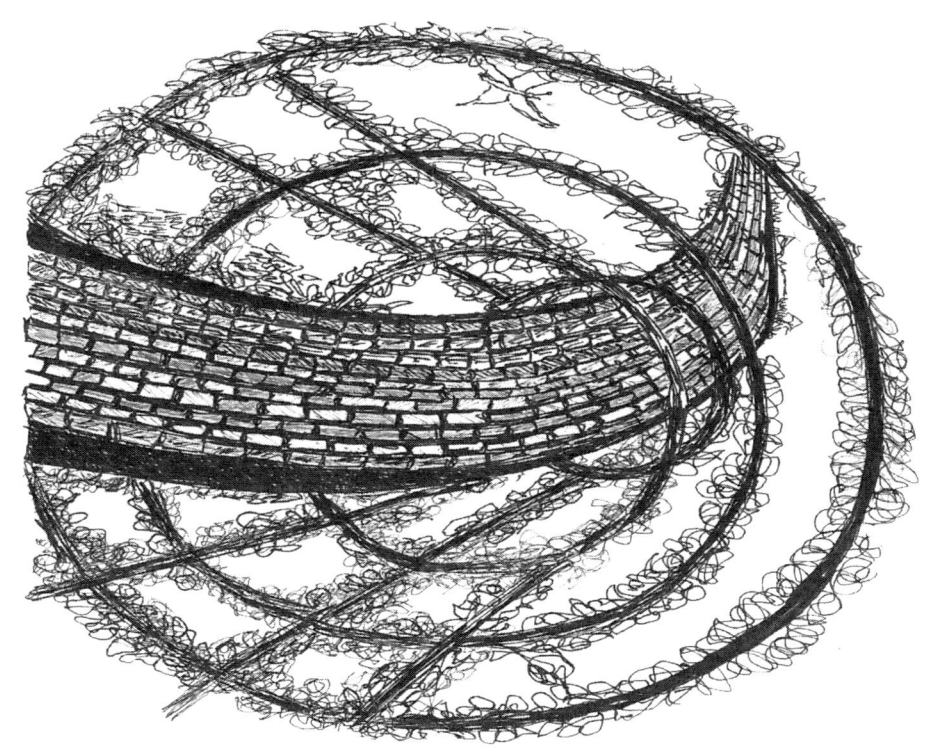

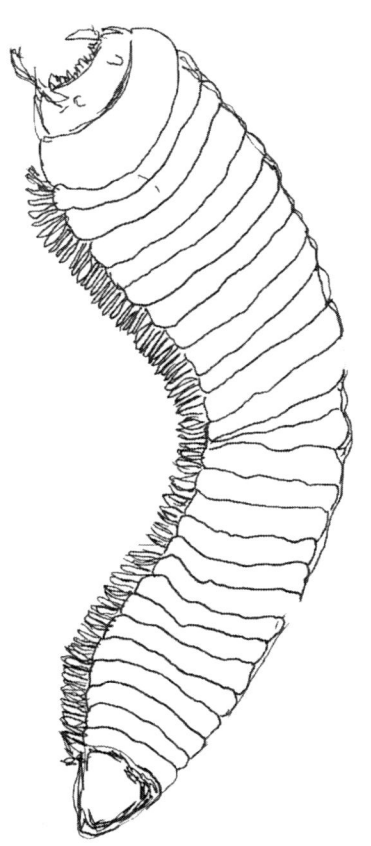

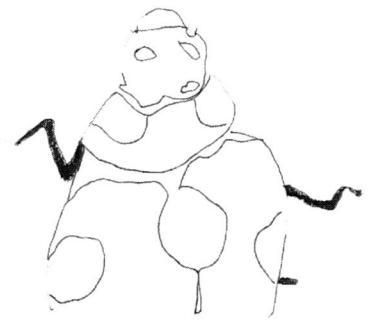

Preying on a Minibeast

How many visual onomatopoeias can you count?

Hands clumsy, curious,

Grab at green furry rock (beneath hedge)

Push it aside to reveal squiggly, squirming grey-black creatures with what looks like zillions of legs.

Spearmint eyes grow into fizzbombs exploding when emptied into Nice Price cola bottles.

Chaos brings one chubby hand down to pick up a juicy and very active specimen.

Whoops – **squeezes** too hard on the shell which confirms invertebrate.

Crunch!

Oh dear. Wipes forefinger along the grain of the grass as if thoughtfully ridding a bogey onto a sort of clean tissue.

Focusses.

Tries again. Finds one sporting a thorax and abdomen sitting on a head next to a dried out blackberry.

Looks around for an accomplice; for affirmation of this moment.

How many legs will it take to convince Mum and Dad that there is a difference between insects and spiders?

Preying on a Minibeast
Doodle your own minibeast wings!

Hands

clumsy, curious,

Grab at green furry rock

(beneath hedge)

Push it aside to reveal squiggly,

squirming grey-black creatures with what

looks like zillions of legs. Eyes grow like

exploding fizz bombs of spearmints

emptied into Nice Price cola bottles.

Chaos brings one chubby hand down

to pick up a juicy and very active specimen.

Whoops – squeezes too hard on the shell which

confirms invertebrate.

Crunch!

Oh dear.

Wipes forefinger along the grain of the grass

as if thoughtfully ridding a bogey onto a sort of

clean tissue. Focusses. Tries again. Finds one

sporting a thorax and abdomen sitting on a head

next to a dried out blackberry. Looks around

for an accomplice; for affirmation of this moment.

How many legs will it take to convince

Mum and Dad that there is a

difference between

insects and

spiders?

Mama Cocoa

My mummy is a cocoa tree.
Understory canopy, mid-height
covered in cacao pods rich
ruby, royal
purple, pine.

On up days her tallness is stunted
branches, sinewy interlocking.
Yet now and then she drops her guard
making space to learn me everything.

Ejecting from her hair threadlike, wiry
stories of giants and cocoa beans tumble
down Mandela's chocolate beanstalk
to melt at my feet of the Johannesburg sunset, humble.

Rustles of Egyptian music
travel down her trunk in waves
exposing ancient scripts playing
dark red roots sunk in a soil of pollinated octaves.

When she laughs all of Mother Nature
ripples in the sweet, pods pulpy softness.
When she tells me off
chips of roasted cocoa
nib my heart.

A switch. A spiral into that hazy fog within herself
a void with cumulonimbus clouds
alerts me to her storm
as she tries to hold me far away enough
not to spy chocolate drops from her eyes.

At those moments
so bitter as to cause Hansel and Gretel's
cacao beans to disappear
her eyes would not blink
her voice would not lilt
her arms rag doll flop.

When she returns she explains that
she needs those spaces
to sit and reconcile
the white and the dark, the clouds against the stark
reality of not being able to uproot herself, to be free to fly.

So I made a camera from sweet memories
and loo roll, stuck to a toothpaste box.
I took a photo of mum and me and placed it gently near her roots.

"Something to take with you when you go away again", I said

"Something to anchor me again?" She accepts.

My answer, "When you dream chocolate tree tales
you will always brood over being grounded.
Copper-tailed starlings will flock to your sweet podded understories
distracting you from the bitterness of the cacao bean."

Builders

There are those with bricks

And those with mortar

There are sticks for boys

And spoons for daughters

There are mudflats

Riding out the shores

There are frames

Within which she hides her cause

There is a sign towards right

A frown facing wrong

There is every flipping

Type of sinful song

That can wring your ears

Until they drum

And make you groan

When she marches on

There is a sneaky glimpse

Of petty aggression

A rhyme to fold -

A punch that reasons

Who fears that luck

Will breed a fierce lady?

Who cares that mum

Will be scorned for the ready?

There are lemons squeezed

Onto colourful stories

There are dragons, liars

And terrible penguins

All will lift a 5-foot ball

Across an alien Derby board

To give her strength and peace of mind

To craft her thoughts.

To save her-kind.

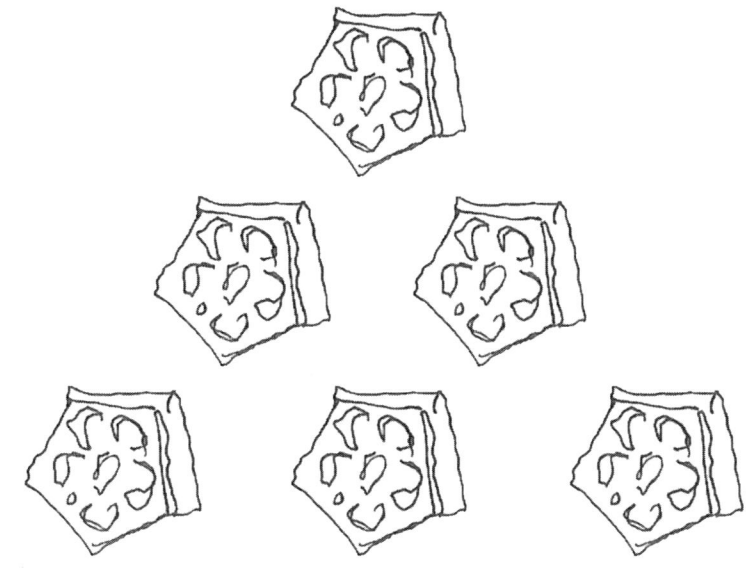

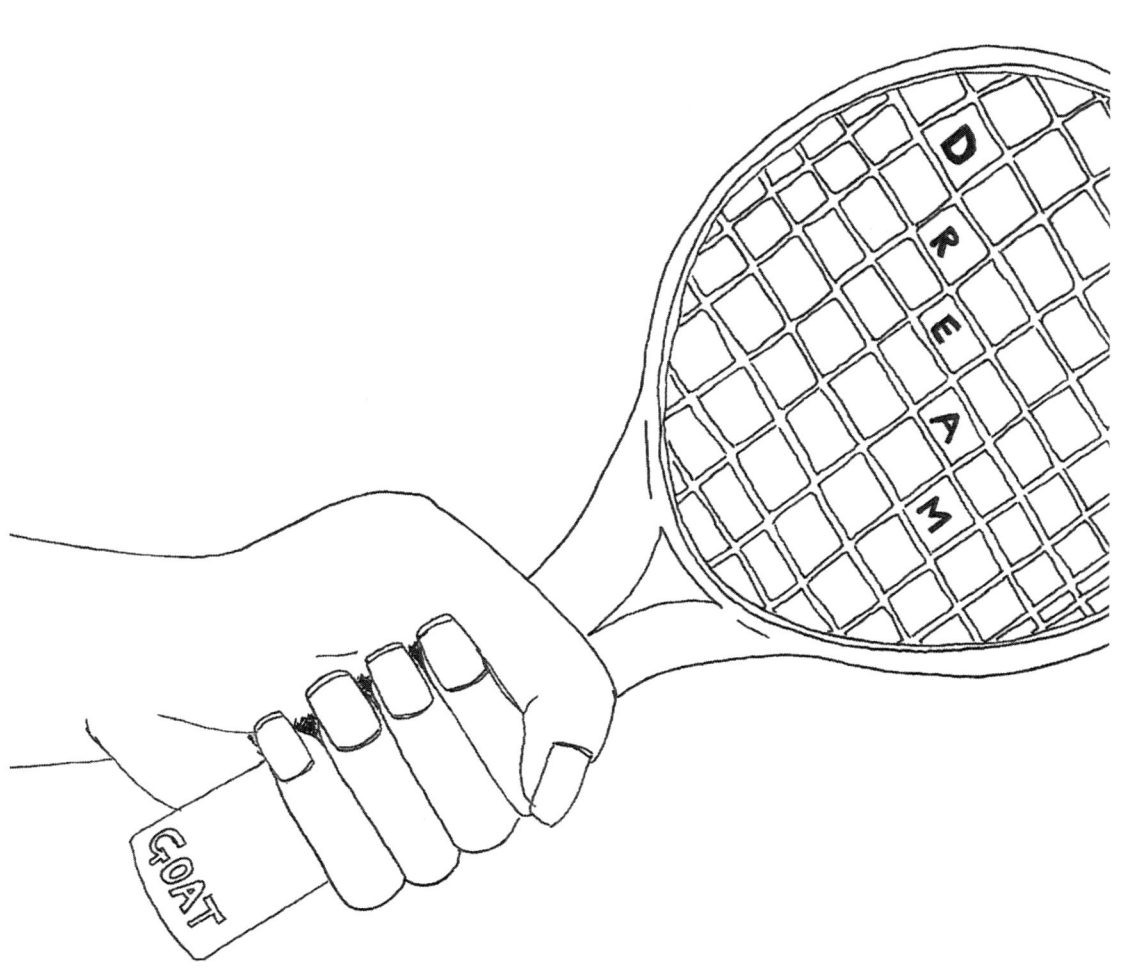

The G.O.A.T.

My 10 year old #son says, "Carry on with your #dreams."

My 9 year old son says, " Every time I watch you I #learn from you."

My 7 year old son says, "Every person in the world
should be allowed to play
#tennis.

It is not about #skin #colour. "

Cromer Beach

We broke our silence with pastels.

Cones stroking waves stroking huts.

We crushed the surf and fixed our hearts

on sunshine, extended family and friends.

So the heavens rained kites

tied

to

ribbons

of

cirrus.

Half Life
The Story

I am a leader

> They see me as great

I deal in open corners

> I am everyone's mate

They trust in my endless supply

> of good stuff, of quality

My prices don't lie

> so I clean up as they flock to me

I make daily corn in break times

> from my peeps with notes to pay for lunch, star

I share my profits with those strays

> I chat sense with my regulars

It's like I feed the five thousand

> but not so others would know

Though I can freeze out some 12 year-old peers

> wanting me to swap biscuit packets for snow blow

I am da king of the timetable

> I fully fund my toasted bagel lifestyle

But my morals won't ride stable

> if I merge into weed and blow

Another layer off the onion

> as pushers know my brown skin

Can shepherd droves of Year 7's in

> it's the status of my melanin.

Punished Valentine

Dying as I touch the thought of you
stood here; a naked mirage
dreaming of those interjecting violins.
Your strings collapse my eardrums
trickle noises that make you murmur,
"Prayers for release". A scatter of your projections -
your neediness - infects my mind.
When your softness is stroked
in circular motions
images of being reborn light up my hands
and I cry out in joy -
a cosy feeling
until my heart
just
stops.

No Hard Feelings

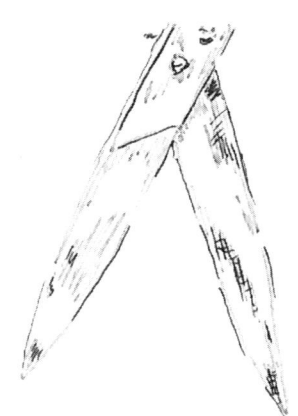

He placed them in little pockets

Sewn by large hands to delicately bind

Leaf-laced pages inscribed with spider scrawls

Chasing needles to furrow his forehead.

In little pockets he placed them.

Lined up against a wall of silence.

Each flap closed with a pop button,

Except the last one, which screamed for attention.

He placed little pockets in them

His knife marked dough swiftly, evenly.

Air, simmering, gave way to space, gave way to sky

The equator limited his freed temper.

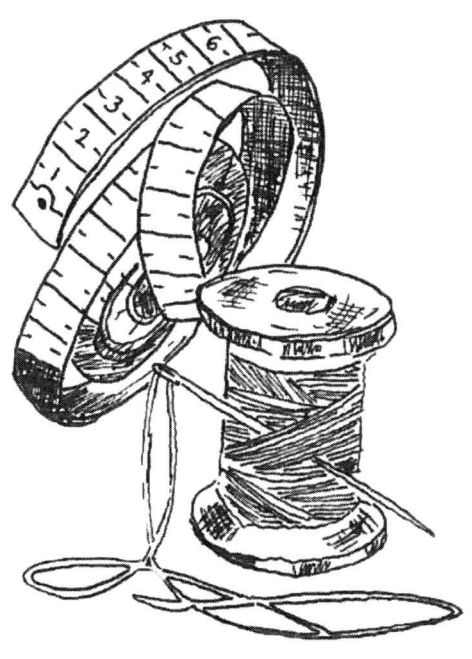

My Uncle Chukwuma

Delivered at my Uncle's Memorial

God knows
You know him too
We know him and what he stood for.
We are market people

From Umuahia

Very simply translated:
Umu - people
Ahia - market

We love people. Talking to them. Working alongside and sharing with
them. We know how to work hard.

He loved to work hard.
I once had an uncle who showed me how to work hard...

Hustle

We hustle to live. To get ahead. To progress. We work hard at the hustle.

Some of us might remember him - or an uncle like him.
He came to live with us for a little while or two when I was a child growing up.

His middle name was Osundu
(Run for your life).
God knows
My Uncle Chukwuma.

A market man from the East of Nigeria who left us unexpectedly at the age of 56.

On 29th March
Travelling from his family home in Lagos.
On a bus.
Going to the east.

Back home, he leaves a handful who will remember him dearly - from 23 years
down to 11.

I didn't know him, but it has been good to find out about him. To share our memories and knowledge about him. This research has brought 3 generations closer together, even if for one day.

We are here because we now know him more

And we know a little bit more about each other

And I feel I know a little more about the culture of the people

Of Umuahia

'Cause he was my Uncle Chukwuma.

God knows.

Doodle...

...design

...and dream...

...your own family crest.

Bag for Life

Standing atop near Mount Inasayama's Observatory

Nagasaki;

bags below my eyes greed fulfillment at the base of Mount Miyajima's shrines.

    Squinting in thirst for the Golden Temple

        and the wooden one

           and the floating one near Hiroshima's shore.

Each shrine is dedicated to each phase of my life.

One plastic bag stretches thinly

to cover a battered good, once freshly wrapped;

    faded hopes fills one declaring 'zip lock';

        reduced-value items weigh down in one lined with crumples.

Decaying carrier bags

    resemble sprinkles

        flaked onto yellow iced cupcakes.

Gently placed, is each cupcake,

    inside a box decorated in cowrie shells and emerald stones.

Procrastination places the box down, unsure of whether to leave it open.

Baggage finally abandoned,

I leave the cupcakes for the eagles to share.

Lift

Performed on stage lying on a yoga mat

"What floor you on?"

She sneered

whilst fake smiling.

Sweat tumbling over her 'Pop Sugar'-

wannabe form.

I was trembling

holding on for dear life

afraid to answer

but knowing that one more thrust

could tip this body

over the edge;

facing a future full of

strained constipation.

and wee-wee leaks

and so I looked through the light
ignoring my grievances
pushing my post-partum form
channeling Serena Williams
who this past weekend
did it for the Wimbledon '18 mums

#IKR

ready to roll over my Down Dog

and push my pelvis from the basement to the penthouse -

an offering to the god Amun-Ra

But.

Maybe not today

as I gazed into my present

and held this moment.

Taking my Serena cape off and
guarding my precious little one
I rolled him off into the sunset

'cos this is the only floor I know.
The one that keeps me grounded.

Excitement

3.59

and one pair of eyes

and the other body in the single bed opposite.

No response.

Repetitive zapping required.

Time now is 4.03

and 3 pairs of eyes dart slits

as feet gently touch cool floor.
Scurrying slippers skate over loose floorboard alarm making a dash for

Bladders emptied, a retreat to bed for another snatch at excited sleep
until the promise can be revealed in the glory of sticky tape

elephant

Whispers of 5.20 echo around the dead of morning as the theta phase
Mum staggers into boys' bedroom and looks at her xenolithic brood.
Her threat to break the promise is spoken.

Eyes, bright with early morning, zap through Mum's sleep.
Three little princes bearing gifts of coffee – no –
school-made cards of a glittery reindeer,
a finger painted tree and a merry sleigh

The promise is delayed by the five-minutes plus 30 of toothpaste and kids telly.
Itchy fingers and whining groans drag Dad and Mum from their spoon into comfy
house clothes.

sends a laser beam to zap one body in the lower bunk

(one pair has spy watch at the ready)

the toilet.

and blinging crackle-effect paper. Mum and Dad roll over and return to

harmonies.

attacks the beta phase.

Not one 'pim' is heard for another 2 hours.

all fight the crumbs of dust gelled to the corners of mum's eyes.

Within seconds of the family gathering and the nod, the promises are ripped into
confetti.

Deep

Cut myself open.

Your love is a lie; absent

I etch into bone. Yes.

High

Notes exchanged for dust

A-sharp enters my nostrils

Grip cotton sheets. Exhale.

Protected

Outside her womb. Noise.

She shields her baby from tales.

He grows polluted

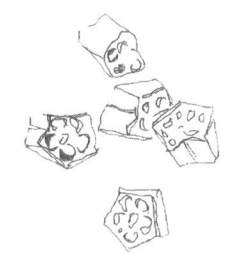

Retro Masquerade

Igbo harmattan

Male's straw skirts beat epic dance.

Tales ground rice in dust

She/They/Me

Female exhibit

Twerk truth; Fashion genitals.

Their mutilation.

Okra Kisses

Mummy you shouted at me

Your voice nailed my feet to earth

Your eyes flint-flashed mango flames

Your teeth spat serrated pearls

Mummy, I can't feel your reach

I can't find your just spirit

I can't trust your hollow mind

Can't taste your okra kisses

Mummy, come hug me please or

Whisper a harmattan breeze?

Can you tickle up my spine?

Can you share again with me

Your kola nut thoughts and rhymes?

Shapes

Flow off polygons and ellipses

that in turn fall from my body's edge.

Which edge?

The mental, the tongue, the fishy orifice or the sole. All are contenders.

My edge is an impossible point to mark,

yet rest assured the geometry

of that mark is ever transient.

If you slide heavy drawers

upon smooth runners,

or pistons pump

an energy cloud

into an impossible space,

what then combusts out

is a magician's bunch

of polyester brights

that light up your smile

revealing multicoloured

silky daisies.

Motherland Masquerade

Skies reflect beamed flecks of ochre
green and blood violet smears
onto ground rice powdered faces
as if the ghosts of minstrels
have arrived to haunt me.

Marks on the sides of cheeks
seem tallied for the count
as they process by each villager, adorning,
yet apprehensive chants
fill the wind dusty with the December harmattan.

Spirits are seen rising
as the red sun sighs on red clay
whoops sound out the retro pattern on djembes;
swollen calves and biceps covered in straw skirts
move my BPM to beats per second.

My cousins take me to the spectators' edge
I shield the skittering of my conscience
placing me behind undressed bushes
to view how the maleness of the masks
vibrate my soul into a trance.

Dust dances viciously
as torsos billow out their bold stories.
Legs akimbo, backs contorting like lizards
a Coca-Cola hat cladded figure
breaks away from his number and dances towards my spot.

Crouched squat I peer through naked leaves
life flares fast before my 14 year old eyes
bright clashes tied around my waist
of an oil palette on starched brocade
signals to this impressive physical storyteller.

As chalked face, straw mask fills my latitude
this onslaught only relieved by
his swollen lips and pronounced nostrils;
breathing escapes my mental ability.
Time begins its prohibition.

Then a coarse horn slaps my eardrums
my feet flip-flop fast towards the others
the masquerade solo jerks away
I turn back to catch the rest of the collective story
and their dances melt into the collected lifedrops
of the night.

see haiku version of this poem Retro Masquerade on p.45

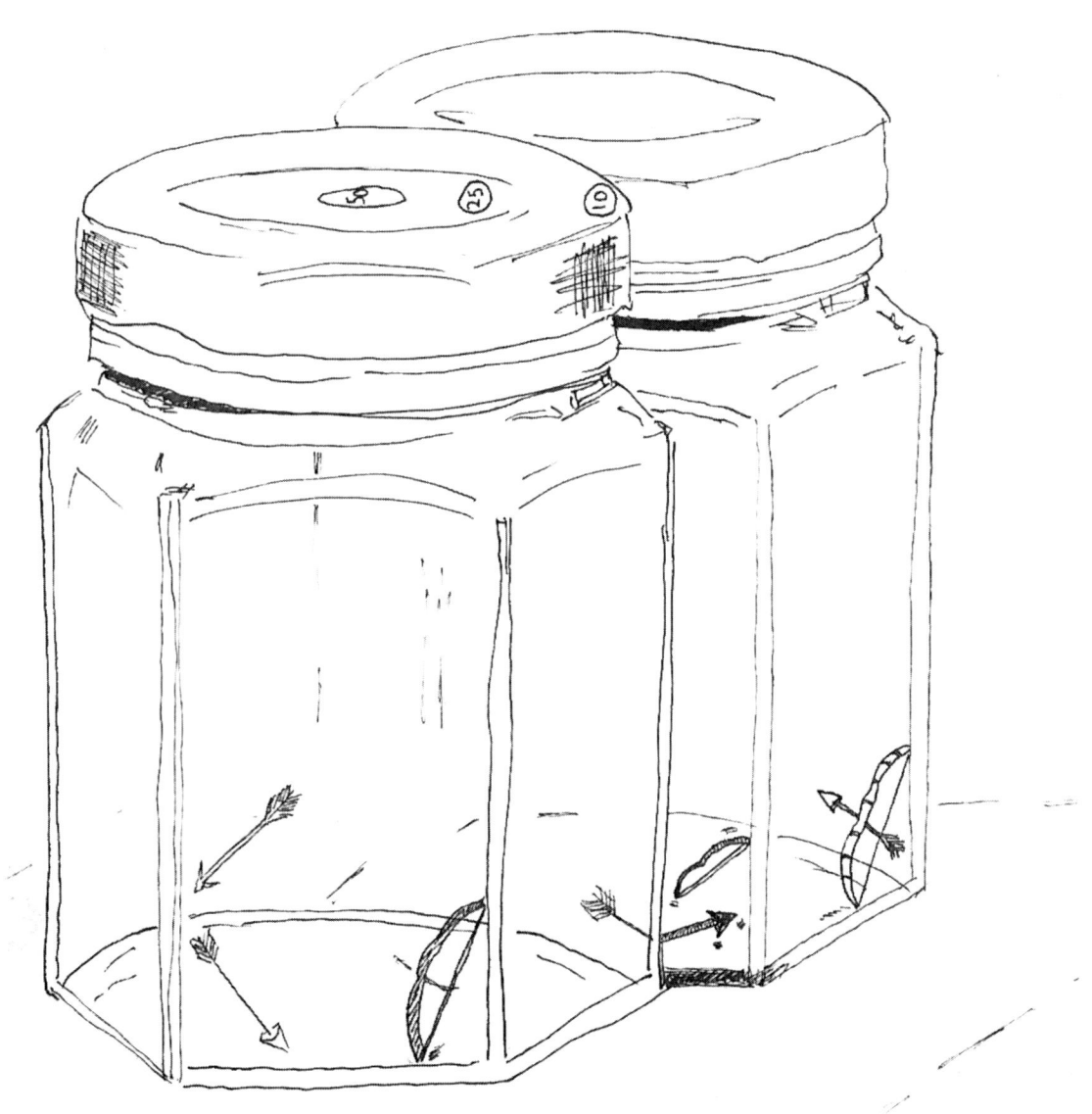

A Child's Dystopia

It was the screams that drew them.

Children hurling decibels from their lungs

Writhing on low branches of chaos

Candyfloss sticking to their exposed skin.

The adults shook their sockets and rolled their lips.

Forming a parachute with empty arms

They called for the children to jump down

They begged them, promising each of them empty honey jars, bows and arrows

They stood broad and deep

Ready to catch any falling stars

And the children laughed themselves into oblivion

All the care in their bodies

Floating upwards

Like the ashes of the phoenix

promised to them centuries ago.

End Notes - Down

Use the clues to fill in the words. Lift your happiness in the horizontal spaces.

1. Breathe fast, excitedly (4)

2. Group yourself with people; act for common good (9)

3. Outside, move playfully on equipment: curly or straight (5)

4. Believe in something true; be you (5)

5. Bring into existence (6)

6. Raise awareness of systems which make one discriminate, not elevate (17)

7. You are black obsidian; your fairness golden; respectful frankincense (5)

8. Invest in your level of pizzazz (6)

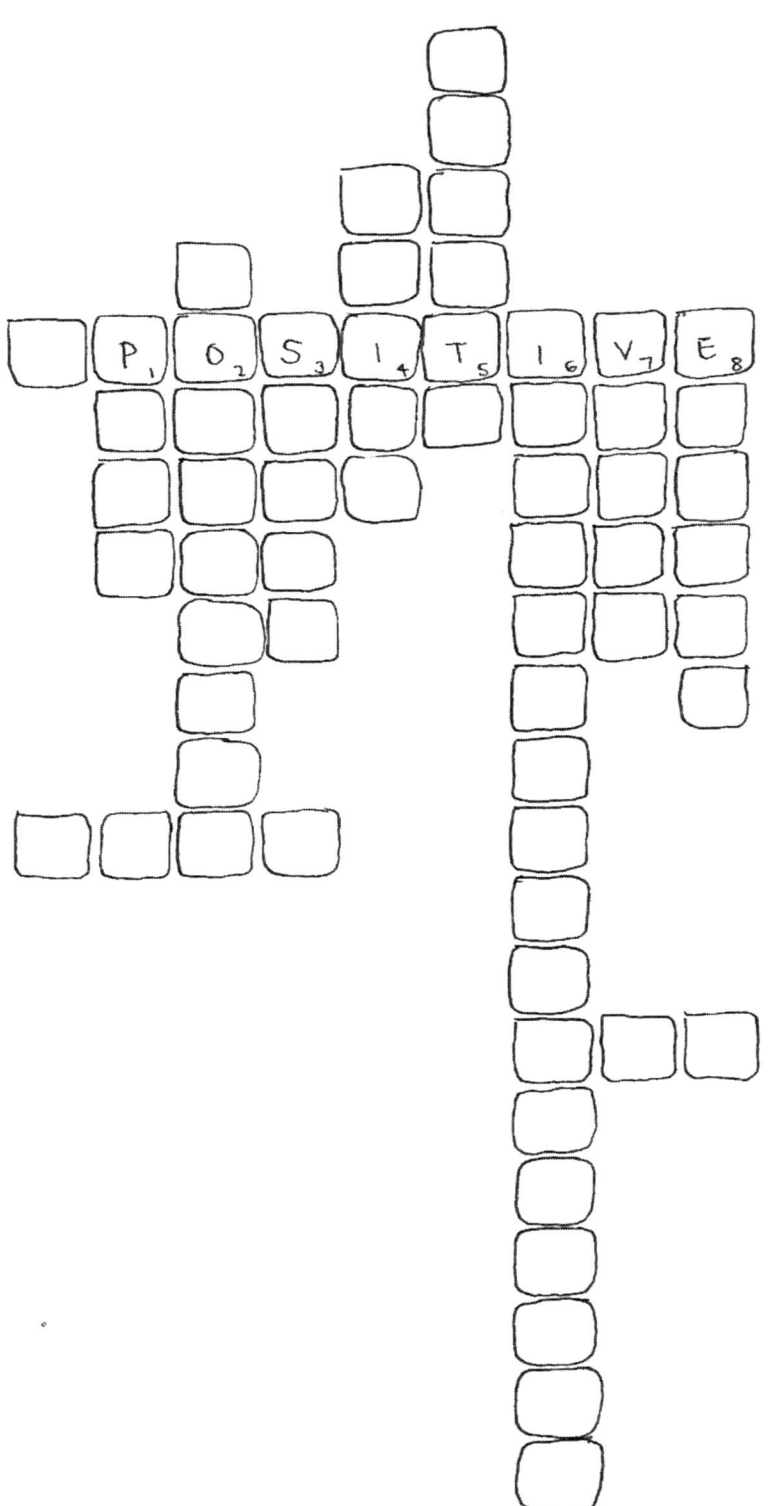

P₁ O₂ S₃ I₄ T₅ I₆ V₇ E₈

Answers (DOWN)

1. PUFF or PANT
2. COMMUNITY
3. SLIDE
4. FAITH
5. CREATE
6. INTERSECTIONALITY
7. VALUE
8. ENERGY